D0397700

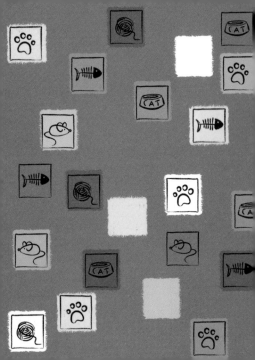

FANG SHUI
Feng Shui for Felines

By Catfucius
With help from Michael Domis

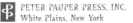

PETER PAUPER PRESS, INC.
White Plains, New York

Illustrations copyright © 2002 Studio 2

Designed by Heather Zschock

Copyright © 2002
Peter Pauper Press, Inc.
202 Mamaroneck Avenue
White Plains, NY 10601
ISBN 0-88088-775-3
Printed in China
7   6   5

Visit us at www.peterpauper.com

FANG SHUI

SHUI

Feng Shui for Felines

"There is great disorder in the heavens— but the cat still naps."

CATFUCIUS SAYS: "The wise cat knows how to be in harmony with its environment. This is the essence of feng shui. A cat enlightened in the ways of feng shui knows how to manipulate its environment to ensure the maximum flow of ch'i (life force). If the cat's desires are met, excellent ch'i is achieved. When the needs of humans and cats coincide, peace and harmony will prevail. When the needs of humans and cats clash, peace and harmony will prevail—for the cat.

"To analyze your environment, use a six-sided map called the paw-gua. The paw-gua shows your position in the known universe. It divides life neatly into six areas. In the north, we find Nature, or the outside world,

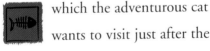 which the adventurous cat wants to visit just after the humans have sat down. To the northeast is the Home, where the cat holds

dominion over all. To the southeast is
Sustenance, or the food that any self-
respecting cat won't eat. South of the
cat is Health, which consists of
copious napping. In the southwest is
Romance, which is slightly more
important than food, but not as
important as napping. Finally, in the
northwest is Family (humans), or
those who think they 'own' cats."

NATURE
Earth: outside litter box
Green: grass to eat
North: to Alaska

FAMILY
Wood: you feed me?
Orange: you glad to see me?
Northwest: is where I'll go if you don't pet me

HOME
Wood: to sharpen claws
White: furniture to shed on
Northeast: direction to sit in

ROMANCE
Fire: passion
Black: of night
Southwest: corner of the house under the bedroom window

SUSTENANCE
Water: to drink
Green: plants to eat
Southeast: place for food bowl

HEALTH
Wood: table to nap on
Metal: desk to nap on
South: auspicious direction to nap in

Do not think of the box in
the corner as a "litter" box.

It is your
Zen garden.

Tilling the garden before and
after planting is relaxing and
will refresh the spirit.

If humans do not refresh the
Zen garden in a timely fashion,
bad ch'i will result.
The wise cat should remind
them to refresh the garden
by planting something where
they least expect it.

Goldfish in the home
make for good ch'i.

They also make a tasty
snack for rejuvenating
flagging energy levels.

Furniture should be decorated in contrasting colors to enhance the flow of energy. If your fur is white, shed only on dark furnishings. If your fur is black, shed only on white furnishings.

Calico cats may shed wherever they wish.

Plants in the northwest corner
of the room create positive
ch'i for the environment.
This positive ch'i is maximized
when the sagacious cat
makes full use of the plant's
energy by eating it.

Care should be taken not
to eat too much of the plant.
This can lead to
excess energy.
You must rid yourself
of this excess.
The wise cat waits until the

dark hours of the morning and
then politely deposits the bad
ch'i where others will be sure
to notice it—for example,
in a bedroom slipper, or on
a newly cleaned Persian carpet.

A solid front gate increases
the likelihood that desires
will be fulfilled. Sit on the other
side of the gate and sing loudly.
In this way, someone will
open the gate, and your desire
to be let in will be fulfilled.

If your desire is simply
to have the gate opened,
gaze longingly into the gate
after it is opened, and
then walk away imperiously
in the other direction.

Once the gate is closed,
recommence singing
until it opens again.

Napping in the correct place is important for tranquility.

Always choose freshly washed, neatly folded laundry to nap on.

Wise cats know how to maximize the tranquil energy of the furniture.

Scrape claws vigorously on the legs and arms of furnishings to create auspicious calligraphic symbols.

Clutter destroys
good ch'i.

Enlightened cats should
eliminate all clutter from
their environment.

To clear a mantel,
walk behind the clutter while
gently pushing it to the floor.
The humans will then
remove it from your space.

Crickets bring good luck.

Bring one into the house.
If it doesn't bring good
luck immediately, eat it,
and get another one.

The inside of the clothes dryer
is warm and inviting, but beware
of fast-approaching humans who
may wish to throw damp clothes
at you and press buttons.

This makes for
very bad ch'i.

You can absorb
energy from many
sources in the home.
The television is excellent
for this purpose, provided
your tail dangles downward
over the screen.

To create good ch'i, a living,
wild creature should be brought
into the house to be played with.
If it dies during play,
however, walk away from it.
Dead things have negative
energy—except when given
as gifts to your owner.

Leaking faucets in the home represent money and energy flowing away.

To keep money and energy
in the home, drink from leaking
faucets. Approach the faucet
from the southwest, taking care
not to dampen your spirit.

Harmony in relationships with humans is essential.

Tell them how much
you appreciate them—
loudly—at 3 a.m.

Energy exits the home
through an open window.
The wise cat will lie in the
open window to absorb
the energy before it leaves.

Mirrors should always be framed to contain their active energy. Unframed mirrors create dangerous energy. The cat reflected in an unframed mirror is an evil doppelganger. Attack it immediately.

The most powerful place
to sit in any room is in
the exact center of the floor,
where you can absorb all the
energy flowing around you.

The pleasant tinkling
of wind chimes
invigorates the soul.

Batting the wind chimes
around at 4 a.m. will
invigorate the soul optimally.

If a room has too much
metal energy in the form of
white furniture, shed on the
furniture to soften the energy.
The gentle curve of a
sleeping cat can also aid
in softening metal energy.

There can be only
one feng shui master
in the home.

Make sure the dog knows this.

Hairballs are bad ch'i.

To transform the negative
energy, deposit them in the
correct corner of the room
according to their color:
orange hairballs in the west
corner; blue in the south; green
in the north; white in the east.

Good grooming makes for good feng shui.

Clean often, paying special attention to the delicate areas of the hindquarters. This must be done in the northeast corner of the room in full view of everyone, especially guests.

When the wise cat is satisfied with the cleanliness of its hindquarters, it should present them for inspection.

Get as close as possible
to the selected guest,
and then swing around
so that he can admire
your clean hind parts.

Sitting on the edge of
the bathtub while it's filling can
help you absorb water energy,
which aids tranquility.

Use caution—falling
in creates a highly
negative kind of ch'i.

If sunlight is not available, heat can substitute.

Occupy the heating vent.
Cover it totally to receive
full benefit.

To achieve the best absorption
of ch'i, always sit on the lap
of the lone human in a room,
or between two humans.
If there are more than two
humans in the room, sit in the
southwest corner and stare at
them. When they glance at
you, absorb the ch'i.

Sharp claws are auspicious.

Sharpen them against
wooden items in the house.
In this way, the tough
properties of the wood are
transferred to your claws.

Cat toys, which represent energy, or the fire element, should be red to stimulate activity and creativity.

Rotate your ears
when necessary to
deflect negative
energy in a more
positive direction.

The wise cat does not nap
with its back to the door.
The wise cat knows that
this is a good way to wind up
stepped on or kicked.

Fu dogs, being made of stone, are excellent protection for the cat. Real dogs are not. Avoid them.

Having a finger pointed or
shaken at you by a human for
something you did is bad luck.
Should this occur,
leave the room very quickly
to avoid the bad luck.

When peace and
tranquility are
achieved, purring
may commence.

The cat strives for grace
and elegance of movement
at all times. Failing this,
act as though any inelegant
gesture was intentional.

Normally, other cats should be avoided.

However, you will eventually desire romance in your life. After finding a suitable mate, romance is best accomplished outside, in the dark, under the human's bedroom window.

The enlightened male cat knows
the best way to entice a female
into his embrace is to sing.
Songs yodeled under
the full moon are
especially favorable
for romance.

An unflattering collar creates bad romance.

The wise cat
knows that all collars are
unflattering. Remove the collar
at once and hide it where
humans cannot find it.

To ensure strong offspring, romance should occur according to fur color. White cats should romance in the winter; orange cats in the autumn; black cats in the spring; tabby cats in the summer. Calico cats may romance whenever they wish.

Cuteness is powerful feng shui—

so powerful that it should only be utilized in the most extreme circumstances, such as when the humans are eating food that you desire, or when the humans think you've done something wrong.

Restore the spirit, when necessary,
by eating the right thing.
Whatever is in the food bowl
at a given moment is not the
right thing. Sit and stare at the
bowl. Eventually, someone will
offer you something else.
Sniff at that, and walk away. Eat
it later when they're not looking.

If served food from a can, it
is inauspicious to eat all of it.
Leave a good portion
to dry out, as a preventive
measure against poverty.

Eating from a
chipped food dish
brings bad luck.

Eat different
prey to enhance
different aspects
of feng shui.

Mice represent domestic
tranquility. Birds allow the
adventurous spirit to take flight.
To enhance sexuality,
take sustenance from a bird
with red plumage.

Catching birds
is good ch'i

However, if the energy you
expend hunting is greater than
the energy received from eating
the bird, it is best avoided.
For this reason, do NOT
hunt hummingbirds.

Be aware that
prey consumed
indoors will affect
your relations
in the home.

Prey consumed outdoors connects you to the external world. Never eat in an open doorway, however, as this represents confusion and can get you stepped on.

There are power places
outside of your home.
Trees are good for their
wood energy, unless you
climb too high and are
unable to get down.

If that is the case,
announce your
predicament,
and help will
appear shortly.

Loud noises are
disruptive to feng shui.

Avoid vacuum cleaners inside
the home, and lawnmowers
outside the home.

Good landscaping is important.

Overgrown lawns are bad feng shui. Eat all overgrown grass.

Use the energy of
the earth to ensure
a successful hunt.

Flatten your body; become one
with the dirt. Feel its power
flowing through you.

Always stalk from your power direction.

Your power direction is anywhere downwind of the one stalked.

When in the garden, savor
the colors of its inhabitants.
Nature's colorful creatures
have great healing properties
and can soothe the spirit
and the stomach.

Property may be marked to insure
that other cats do not trespass on
your space. Mark copiously
beginning in the southwest
corner and continuing clockwise
until finished. The wise cat does
not mark the dog, however,
even if it is outside.